Haunted Southern Nights

Vol. 2

The Haunted Backyard

Written by: Deborah Collard, RN

Haunted Southern Nights

Volume 2 – The Haunted Backyard

Copyright © 2007 by Deborah Collard

ISBN 978-0-6151-8770-9

All rights reserved. No part of this book may be reproduced or utilized in any form or by any means, electronic or mechanical, including photocopying, recoding, or by any information storage or retrieval systems, without permission in writing from the publisher. For information contact: Deborah Collard at nealparasociety@aol.com
Printed in the United States of America
Cover Design by Deborah Collard

Acknowledgments

Haunted Southern Nights as you know is and will continue to be my dream that is slowly turning into a reality. My first book Haunted Southern Nights Vol. 1 Ghost Hunting, the Basics+ was published early last fall. Now I ask you to continue this journey with me in Volume 2, The Haunted Backyard.

I want to acknowledge my wonderful family: my husband Greg, my daughters Barresa and Ricci, my son Brandon, my Mother Dioma, my grandchildren Mikie and Kaylee. I love them all so very much and they give me the time and space I need to follow my dreams and encourage me not to hold back. If I've heard once I've heard many times, "It makes no difference what other people think Mom, go for it!" And I do, time and time again.

I have so many friends and colleagues to say thank you too for all the support they have given me and how they continue to be supportive and love me no matter what the case may be. Then entire staff of North-Eastern Alabama Paranormal Society: Nathan Levan, Larry Hydrick, Brandy Craig, Ricci Guess, Robert Atchley, Barresa Guess, Stacey Adams, Kim Barker, Patrick French, Dave & Lynn Spiller.

A very special thank you for those of you who have been my closest friends throughout these special years of my life: Patrick Burns, my mentor, you know I love you! Your belief in my talents has encouraged me more than you will ever know. Dave Schrader, you can make me laugh when I think the whole world is coming down on me. Cari Stone, girl you know exactly how to pick me back up and make me smile! Reese Christian, you my dear are the closet thing to a sister I could ever want, I love you. Maybe someday you'll get me to refer to my gift as the "P" word but not this week. Jana VanDyke, here I go again and you are right there to encourage me on.

To all the Paranormal Investigators I have trained in the Haunted Backyard, I say it's been worth it to me. Not only did you learn but you gave me the pleasure of being a mentor to you.

To all the Paranormal Teams who have investigated the Haunted Backyard, you see you weren't crazy; you really did see and feel all those paranormal things. Little did you know you were validating many events that have occurred with your own evidence?

To any paranormal investigator who wants to investigate the Haunted Backyard, I say "come on!" See if you can answer some of the questions I have.

To all of you that I love and respect, you bring much joy to my life and I will be forever grateful.

Much Love,

Deborah

Dedication

This Volume of Haunted Southern Nights is very humbly dedicated to my Mother, Dioma Parker. Mom, I know I don't call you as often as I should, I know I don't visit as much as I should, but I love you with all my heart. These gifts that I've been blessed with are a part of you, a special part. Without your ongoing guidance and love I would not be complete.

        Love, Your Daughter,

            Deborah Ann

Table of Contents

The Smothering

The Night We Sang

Sarah and Her Smile

Fairies Fly

The Introduction of Mary

Crossing Over

Aliens

Give Me a Sign

The Little Green Man

The Indian Princess

Dousing Validation

Vortex or Not

Lay Lines

The Finding of Bones

Dancing Lights

The Native Americans of the Woods

The Flight of Zeus

The Power of the Circle

The Empowering Trees

Hell's Path

Sing Louder to Me

Twas the Night Before Halloween

Spirits Riding Through

Demonic Banishing

When the Candles were Lit

I'm Watching You

Faces Watch Too

Are Children More Aware

Deborah's Ghostly Family

Orbs that Trail Along

Red Orbs

Hexagon Shaped Orb

(Mist)ical Photos

I Ask Myself Why?

Tidbits of Information of Meltonsville

The Smothering

It was a cold night in the old backyard. My husband, a friend and I were enjoying a nice fire in my circle. It was a full moon and at that time I choose to honor the spirits of my beliefs. We were all laughing, just enjoying good fellowship and it came time for me to get up and light some white sage and bless the area. While doing so I called upon the 'good spirits' to come forth. Little did I know there was more lurking about that were not so good. As I began talking to the spirits in the way I do, I began feeling like there was a presence about, an unkind one. My husband was taking photographs this night of everything, including me. All at once I began having difficulty talking while standing over the picnic table. Instead of running up to me, he began to take photos. The difficulty in talking turned into being smothered. I asked for help. It seemed like an eternity before someone got to me. I had begun to go down on my knees to the cold ground. I was helped to a bench. It took me about five minutes to regain my thought processes. I suffered a total lack of energy, as though the very heart of me had been taken right out of my body. Fear, I felt fear. My breaths as they returned to normal were feeding my lungs. I can't remember ever having felt so hopeless. As soon as I could muster the strength I made my way inside. I laid down on the couch to rest. I continued to do so for two days. I managed to take a bath in sea salts in hopes that whatever had happened to me would be eased out of my body and the healing process would begin. On the second day I decided to upload the photographs that were taken that night. At the moment I had begun to feel as if I was being smothered there it was. It appeared to be a type of round shaped object concealed partially by my face yet the mist of it ran around my neck. Yes I was being attacked or attached upon by someone or something. To this day I am not certain which. All I know is that from then on I became a much more cautious investigator even in times of pleasure. One never knows when or why these things happen to us, but it did me. You can see if for yourself in the following photograph.

Colorful Orb with gray mass encircling my throat.

"The Smothering" as I call this occurred February 24, 2005. I don't know why it wanted to hurt me, but it did. My face is not even visible for the mist enveloping my mouth and neck. As for the orb, I'm not sure if it had a connection or not, but the color of it is unusual and very solid green.

The Night We Sang

You know how it is when the girls get together. It was night of acting foolish and loving every minute of it. Do you remember singing with your friends driving down the road or around a campfire? Well it was another fun night in the backyard. I, along with a couple of girlfriends was enjoying a bit of sharing of the song, so to speak. While the singing was going on, so was my camera. Do you know what it means to get 'your hackles up'? Well when my dog does his hair stands straight up on his back. Mine did this night on my neck. I felt like we were not alone, so I was snapping pictures left and right trying to get a glimpse of something. Then out of my peripheral vision I could see something black in motion. I swung around and took several pictures and too my surprise after uploading them found this.

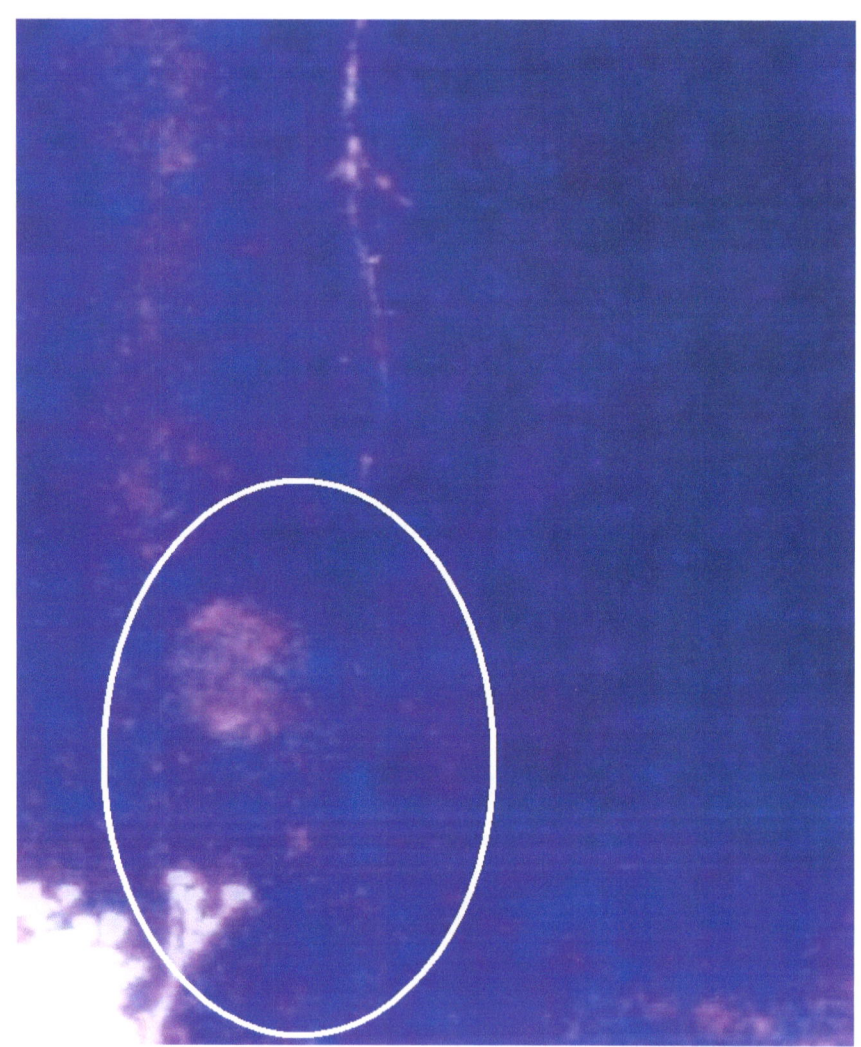

22

I don't know if you see her the way I do, but she has the most solemn look on her face. Her face voices sincerity, she's one with complacency and most important one with curiosity. The lady appears to be middle age, with black hair and almost Celtic in appearance. That night we were singing Celtic songs. I don't know if you believe in miracles, but I do and it was a miracle to see this lady join us on a girl's night out singing in the backyard. From the appearance of her cape I would think her to be of someone who might have lived in the early 1800's. She might be residual haunting or someone just passing through and was drawn to the singing. One does not truly know, does one?

Sarah and Her Smile

Sarah, as we lovingly call her has been a regular in the backyard for the last 16 years. Sarah seems to depend upon me to be there for her at least a couple of times a month. If I don't show up in the backyard, things seem to start happening inside the house. Believe you me I know when its time to make an appearance. Sarah is quite the communicator too. She will make an Electromagnetic Field Detector go wild and will chatter up a storm while I'm using dousing rods. Here is Sarah.

Sarah leads us to believe she's around 11 years old. Sarah leads us to believe that she will never cross over, that she is indeed very happy just where she is. So, I don't push it. I let her stay. I mean, how could I stop her if I tried? I never go into the backyard without telling Sarah that I love her. Ok, so I talk to ghosts? She's a very special to my heart. Many people have sensed her presence and I'm sure many more will to come. In the photos that Sarah has been captured in she tends to wear the same era of clothing, estimated seventeenth century. I don't know who she really is, but I can live with that. Sarah reacts differently to different investigators. At times she can be almost fearful but she seems to be a beacon if trouble is about. She seems to sense it and lets us know.

Fairies Fly

Ok, I'm going right out on a limb here, but I'm a paranormal investigator, I do it daily. Do you believe in fairies? Well I kind of 'do'. Sometimes you can see lights in the woods and they are not lightening bugs, they are much larger, softball size. Well on this one particular night in the backyard while I was training some new paranormal investigators I captured a picture of what appeared to be a 'gold orb'. Well that intrigued me to begin with, but when I actually looked more closely at the photograph I could see many things but the thing that stood out the most was the appearance of wings. Now I will share "Goldie" with you.

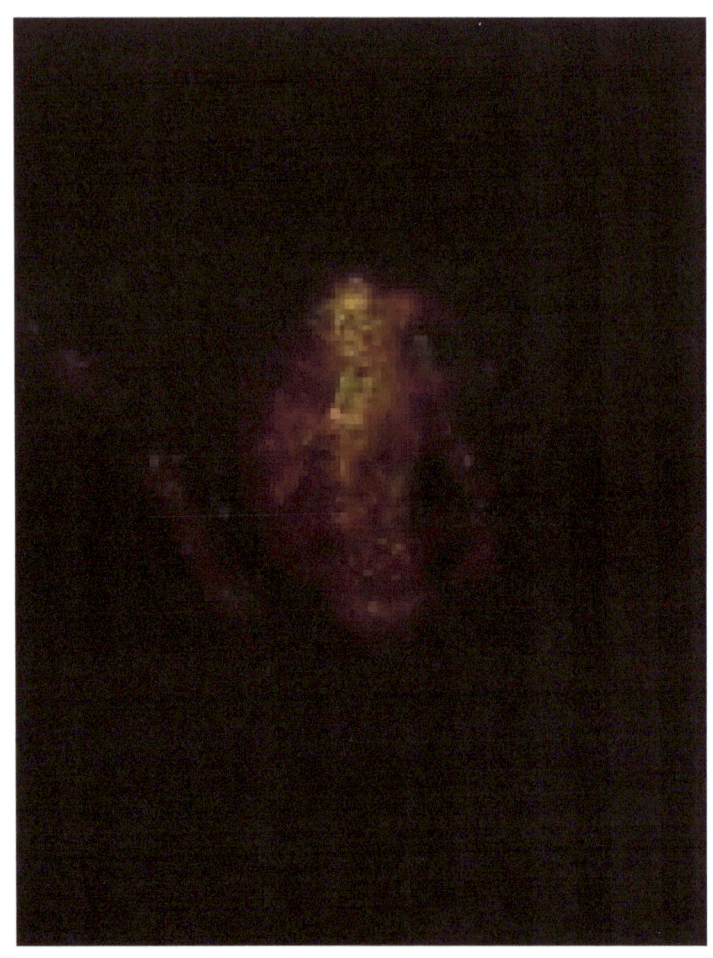

"Goldie" is definitely not your everyday Orb. I've studied orbs for years and never once I have come across this type of anomaly before and I have not again

since this one time. I've heard people comment they could see many things in this photo. But it was just an orb I thought. The color is why I looked deeper. Goldie did not have to be enhanced or worked on to bring 'it' out. You be the judge of what you see, but it the closest thing to a fairy I've ever seen in my life other than a real life moth that I've seen that remarkably resembles a miniature Tinker Bell. And when I say resembles, I'm quite serious. These moth type creatures will literally send out a "scout" if I may be so blunt and they will actually fly right up next to you and observe you, allowing you to look at them. I think you get too "in awe" to move and then they flutter away as quickly as they came. I really didn't want to tell this one, but for the sake of paranormal science I am. And no, I'm not nuts yet; other people have seen them as well.

The Introduction of Mary

There is a path in the woods that leads to a place where the K2 meter and other electromagnetic field detectors go crazy. It's a place where I discovered Mary. Mary is an old soul. Mary I believe to be of Native American Heritage. Mary when questioned via dousing rods and K2 meters has responded yes to many questions in reference to Native American lifestyles and healing. Mary is believed to be back there to protect those who are quite possibly buried in those woods from centuries past. She controls those woods I tell you! This is the one capture I have of what I believe to be Mary and she was strong enough to appear during the daylight hours.

Now my friends, I don't care who you are but you know it takes a tremendous amount of energy to form, but to capture her in the daylight? Now this was wild, but the Backyard normally is. Mary has warned me many times as well as warned other investigators if she feels danger about. Somehow she can literally make you sick to your stomach, make you have chills that you just can't believe, make the temperature drop drastically, just do all kinds of things to get your attention. Then when you evaluate the evidence "old Mary" was doing her thing. She was taking care of us.

Crossing Over

Yes, believe it or not, there does come a time when I have to muster the energy to assist a spirit in crossing over. I have had people come to me knowing they had something or someone attached to them and it appears that the Backyard houses some type of vortex that enables me to assist with this endeavor. Since being able to do this particular chore in the backyard I have grown accustomed to the manner in which to do this and have been able to accomplish this on several occasions over the last sixteen years and will continue to do so as the need arises. It seems that sometimes spirits get 'stuck', they simply don't know how to follow the light or their fear keeps them from doing so. It's up to people like me that are willing to give all the energy they have to help. I go into an altered state of consciousness and am able to visualize who needs to crossover and even at times who is waiting for them in the light. It's so amazing to see the colors rush by as a spirit runs to the light. To me, this particular one of my gifts is probably the biggest blessing. I thank the creator for it. The Backyard has taught me many things and continues to do so regularly. I have a picture to share at this time that is not of me assisting in a crossing over which would be too private, over but of a very special pet, Rosey. Rosey was shot and killed. I buried her in my backyard. This photo was taken forty-five minutes following the last bit of earth covering her. Don't ask me why I took the picture, I just felt compelled.

I will just say the Backyard holds many secrets. Rosey was a Red Lab Mix. I loved her so dearly. I cried for weeks and still to this day think of her very often. Life and Death work in mysterious ways and I think this was her way of letting me know she would always be with me.

Aliens?

Well where do I start here? I guess I'll share with you a couple of stories. On one occasion I actually have a photograph of 'something'. This was several years back, the backyard was especially active. Not only were those bloody large softball lights going off all over the place, but even the sounds of the animals were different. Extremely loud at times they were then totally silent. You know after you live in a place for such a long time and you investigate religiously in the same location to find answers you get in tune with the entire existence that surrounds it. Let me show you this picture and you decipher what you think it is.

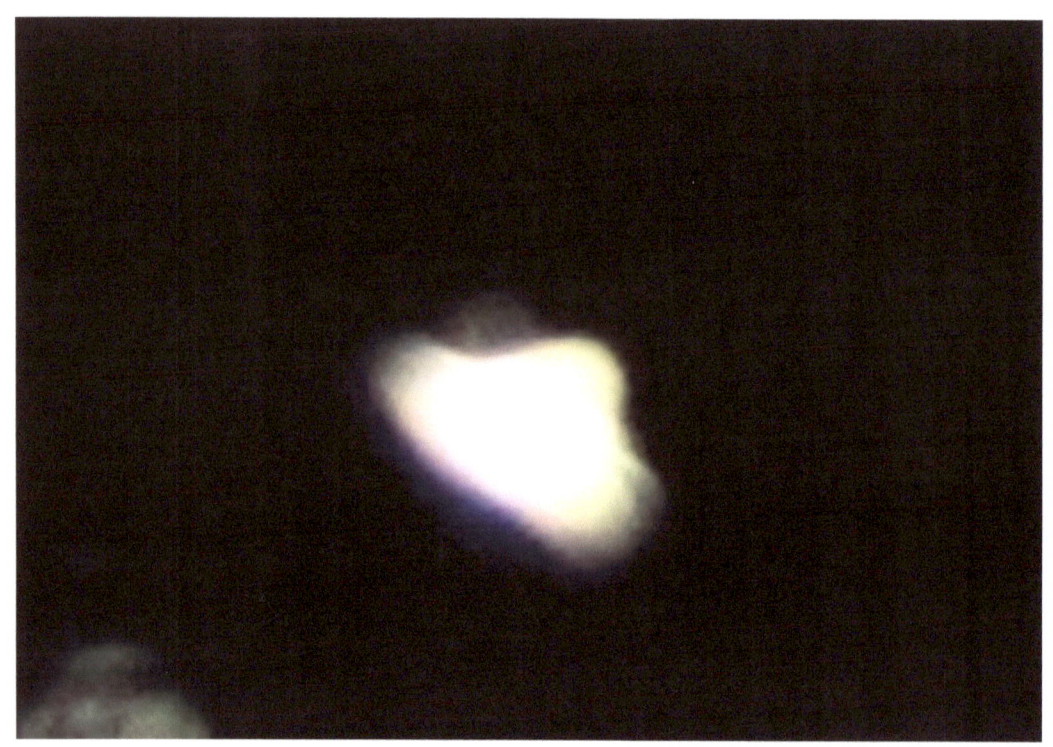

Well I see something on a glowing "something". That is quite the description! If you look closely you can see a round head, unfortunately almost green in color with two very large eyes. What energy or cloud it's riding on or hiding behind is beyond me. I can't for the life of me figure it out. I have tried many ways and times to recreate this picture and just can not do it. It behooves me as to what it is.

On another occasion while I was away, my team was here allowing another paranormal team from out of town to visit and investigate the backyard. In their final report, one of their team members, who were extremely credible, reported having seen an unidentified flying object near the front yard area.

On one particular night while doing a training session in the backyard for paranormal investigators we were snapping photos. We were practicing the take three to five shots at the same location in concession to see if there are any changes in the photos. While doing so we managed to capture something, still to this day unsure of what it was but it was very tall, glowing white, had those slanted alien type eyes and appeared as shocked to have its picture made as we were of getting the photograph.

I'd think I'd be silly to believe that we are the only life that exists in this universe. I mean our moon is a star with all the planets we know of revolving around it and our planet can sustain life so with all the billions of stars in the universe surely there are some that function the same way and can sustain some form of life. I know that I've read many a story about UFO sightings in my area. Some I remember more clearly than others. I know that you all have seen or heard something about a UFO sighting in your area.

The saga of the backyard continues....

Give Me a Sign

Mercy doodles this story is gross! When you ask for something or someone to give you a sign of their presence, be careful of what may happen. There were five of us in the backyard. I was using my dousing rods. I was asking if there would be spiritual activity that particular night. Then I asked if there was already someone there. THAT question came out of my mouth while using the rods, "If there is someone here, would you give me a sign? Would you please do so without causing harm to anyone who is with me?" About that time, out of no where, I mean no where I was engulfed by flies! Yes, flies! I hate flies!!! They were all over me.

Five people standing there, two to my left and two to my right and I am squealing for someone to please get them off of me. Flies are absolutely the nastiest things to me and I assure you I had had a bath. But I got my sign, oh heck yes I did. I am very cautious about when I ask that question now. You just never know what you will get when you ask.

The Little Green Man

I have tons of pictures of this fellow, but I'm greedy with him. My NAPS team has seen so many its not funny. He's like our staple in the backyard, ever present. You never know what shot or video he's going to be in but you can rest assured he will show up. I can think of countless nights following training when we have all anxiously waited, after uploading pictures onto our laptops for the appearance of the Little Green Man. We all laugh. We all just love to see him come up. Too funny!

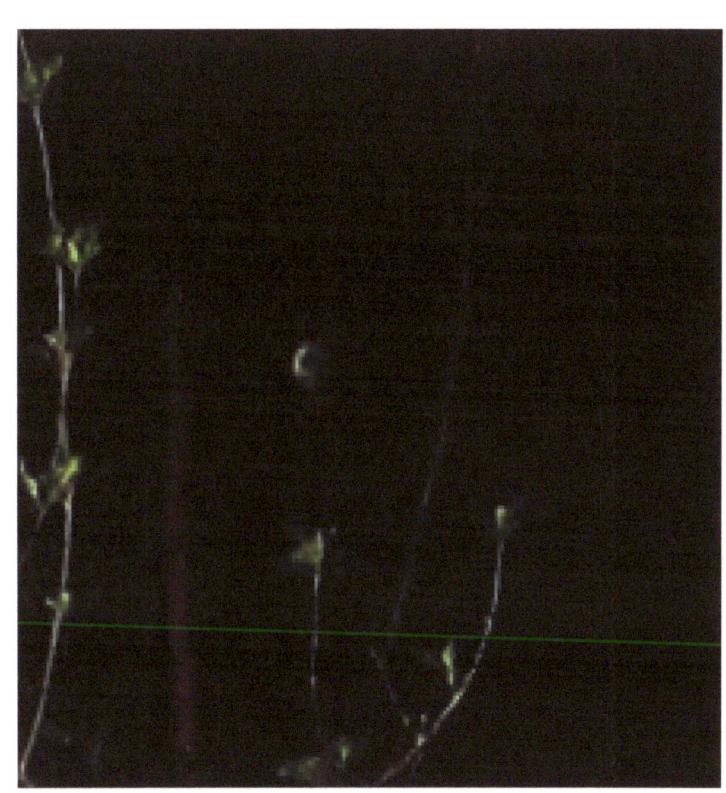

The Indian Princess

At least that's what I call her. One night about five years ago I walked out into the backyard and without any ado I started making photographs, one right after the other. I know I took a hundred photographs. I had been sitting in the house and had 'the itch' to get out there. It's almost like someone is having a party and they forgot to invite you so you invite yourself. Well it's my backyard so I invited myself. Was it a grand night or what? I caught this gal off guard. I tried for weeks to make her NOT be there, but to no avail. She was there and very real. Here are a few shots of her in various formats of trying to eliminate her.

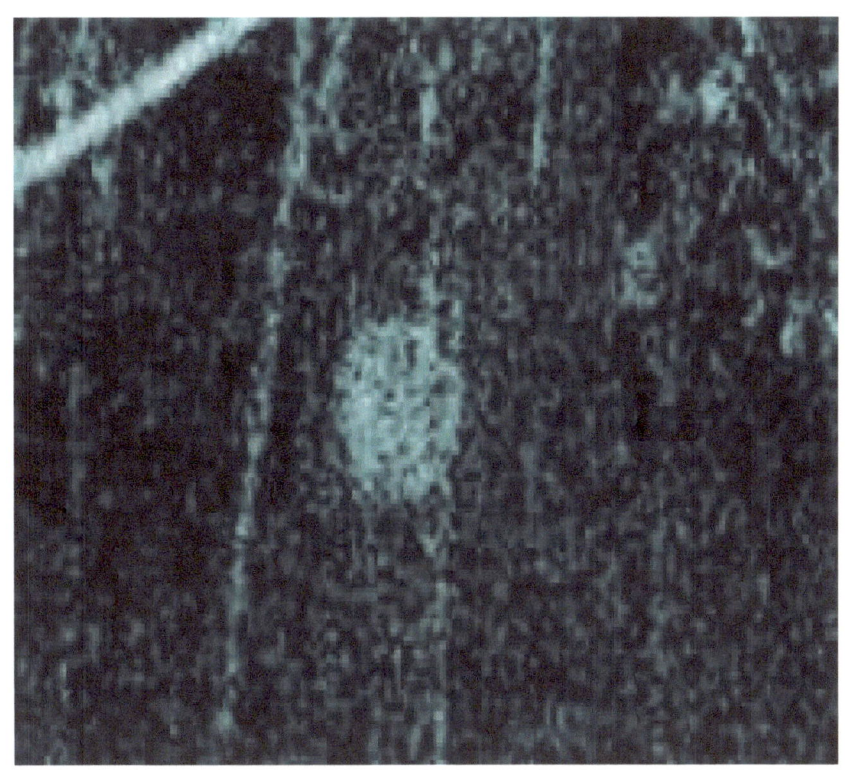

I think she's quite beautiful myself. What do you think?

Dousing Validation

I've told you about my father and what he taught me about dousing rods in my first book. Getting validation with other electronic devices is another thing altogether in the field of paranormal investigation. That was achieved in the Backyard. After our team acquired its first K2 meter, when the dousing rods were hot, so was the meter. It was amazing to see that the rods work with spiritual entities as well as electronic devices. They call me the 'dousing queen'...Too funny. But I would almost put them up against any tool out there for paranormal investigating.

Vortex or Not?

I have heard over the years not only the scientific definitions through quantum physics all the way to the opposite end of the spectrum of speculation of one being a spiritual doorway. Now being the person I am and trying to understand how this term evolved into paranormal investigations makes some sense however, I'm just not sure it applies. Maybe we should come up with our own 'word'. When I think vortex, I think a tornado or hurricane even as far as shape. You know as well as I do that those are swirling winds moving in a circular manner where at different levels there are different levels of electromagnetic readings. These monsters of weather phenomenon make us stand up on our toes and pay attention. They can be the culprits that create everything from mass hysteria to catastrophe. Well now how does this apply to my backyard? At times there are a couple of different locations where you feel like you are being enveloped in energy. The hair on your arms rises as though you've just taken clothes out of the dryer and they have static electricity to the degree the clothing pops on your skin while pulling then out of the dryer and even while pulling one article of clothing away from another. That feeling of energy does appear to have motion to it. Would I call it swirling? Yes and No. You can definitely as I said feel movement but since you cannot visualize it with your naked eye it makes it difficult to determine whether you would consider this paranormal activity a vortex. I feel like it would be a stretch to use the term, but there are significant changes that cannot be ignored, therefore I have no choice but to use the term. I would prefer to use the word 'portal'. You ask why? To me a portal is also a doorway. It's a more a dimension of time where spirits choose to walk. I know this is a nit picky subject but I don't mind giving my opinion. It's my belief that sometimes spirits meander for reasons unknown to us. Maybe they simply have unfinished business, maybe they don't think they'll make to the heaven they've been taught about, maybe they think they will end up in purgatory, maybe they are simply scared for no reason. I further believe that at times they reach an area in this journey where doorways will open that correspond with the dimensional planes through some type of electromagnetic shielding that breaks down or is weakened for some reason and we as investigators are able to capture their images or feel the pain they suffer or even they have the capability of communication in some form. Now don't ask me how I can scientifically justify what I have just stated, as I said this is my opinion. In my heart I believe that when faced with ghostly entities that they fear us as much as we fear them. Take the theory of aggression from nature. Animals don't normally under normal circumstances attack humans unless they feel threatened. An animal can detect danger from sounds we can't hear, feelings that we don't pronounce that our bodies give off and also you have to consider their protection mode. Ok, all this rambling and what does this have to do with Vortices. Well I'm just not convinced that Vortex is the proper term, although I have seen photographs of what appear to be vortices, but what do they have with spiritual entities? I believe them to be solely scientific and based on electromagnetic and electrical doing. On the other hand Portal behavior to me is similar in some ways and more defines what we face when doing paranormal research. With that said, I'll hush about it since I know we all have our own opinions. Some of you may share mine. But with my Backyard, this is my conclusion.

Lay Lines

Lay lines are said to be areas that there is a tremendous amount of spiritual energy. It is said also that many a holy temple or building are built upon these lines. To me from what I've read, I perceive them to be the perfect location for a haunting. These lines have been drawn out and etched on maps for centuries. I know not whether the backyard sits on a lay line but I do know that in certain areas where there should NOT be electromagnetic fields, there are.

The Finding of Bones

This is a story told as factual by a local, a neighbor, who has lived on this road since back in the 1950's. A few years back I had a discussion with this neighbor about the "activity" in the backyard area. Her response was "well probably so". She knew that I was of Cherokee Blood and told me this story and here's how it went. Back in the early 50's a couple of men were hunting where now IS my backyard. They came across some human remains, partially exposed. Doing the right thing they reported it and followed up. Back then you could have bones removed and returned to their resting place. Both were educated men. The bones were said to be that of a Native American. The bones were returned to the exact location of their finding and re-interred into the sacred ground from which they were removed and the grounds re-blessed. So you see there is most likely a burial ground right out my window. I know not of the extent of the burial ground nor do I choose to dig to see. All I know for certain is I'm proud to be so close to my people and honor them by neither excavating "Nor" removing one tree.

Dancing Lights

I bet you are wondering what this is. I know, it's my own set of words, but brought together for a reason. Some nights you can sit in the backyard and observe lights dancing in the woods and NO it's not lightning bugs. I'm a country girl and I know the difference. If you capture them on camera, they are brilliant colors, sometimes red, sometimes purple, and sometimes gold. On one particular night they were as large as light bulbs and more brilliant that a hundred watt bulb. I've asked myself a thousand times, how this could be. I don't know but it can. When you see the really large ones they seem to float like clouds of light and then fall and fade. Where they go, I know not. Where they come from, I know not. I only know they exist and they are not bugs or fireflies. Someday I will discover what they are, I just know it. Do you want to know a secret? I think they are those fairy like 'things'. In fact, the last time I saw them I was also paid a fluttering visit by one of the fairy creatures.

The Native Americans of the Woods

Oh this is something I love to talk about. I feel so protected back there but occasionally something happens that makes me a tad bit uncomfortable. I will give you a prime example. During a training meeting my staff and I went to the backyard and began doing a routine investigation. We try to follow protocol to the letter when possible. We went up into the woods and began doing EVP's (electronic voice phenomenon) and taking K2 meter readings, Infrared Temperature readings, making photographs and of course me and my dousing rods. While in this particular area I could visibly see three Native American males. Then someone else saw them. Then there were two and then I began to feel them draining my energy, my whole body was beginning to tremble. The four investigators back there (Larry, Patrick, Nathan and Robert) saw what was going on. We are so good together we can read what's going on. They guarded me like I was the quarterback, attempting to keep away oncoming evil players. We all stood our ground we did. I spoke rather harshly to these trespassers of spiritual energy and eventually they left. But while they were there we did get a bit of evidence.

I'm sure you can see those "red" faces near the top of the picture. The first picture is totally untouched. They showed up that night in more than one picture. The second on is cropped for you to get a closer look.

Those fellows were keeping an eye on us for quite some time. I get the impression that they are some type of protective force for these woods. They have a permanent place and are accepted by me as the guardians.

The Flight of Zeus

This takes us back to the night of August 1, 2007. This night was rather eventful if I do say so myself. Following a shoot at Sloss Furnaces in Birmingham I had invited Patrick Burns, a dear friend and colleague to come up and check out 'The Backyard'. Patrick was obliged as for years he'd heard many tales coming from myself and other NAPpers. I guess you could say he was curious to see for himself. We arrived back to my house sometime in the early afternoon. We sat and chatted about how things had gone over the weekend and what would be expected to occur in the backyard in relation to paranormal activity. I was as honest as I could be with a "you just never know", but it was going to be another very 'odd' night out there. To interject, I personally believe that the area back there tends to know when strangers are present and seems to have some sense of whether there is anything threatening about.

Zeus who is my Great Pyrenees, a big hunk of white furry love is no stranger to all that goes on back there. For example, Zeus meets me daily as I arrive home from work and runs directly back through "hell's path", around through the back yard and meets me at the steps. Let's just say he's done his 'all clear' for his master.

Zeus had greeted Patrick and I earlier and immediately liked Patrick right off the bat, which was cool. So when darkness began to fall Zeus was more than happy to head out to the backyard with us. To begin with I gave Patrick a tour of the area back there and pointed out key locations although you can see worn paths where for years many have ventured. I built a fire pit many years ago and have it surrounded by five benches built up on concrete blocks so that a group can sit around the fire. To the North I have a picnic table with many objects that I adore placed in locations of my choice. I also have an array of candles in place. We'll talk more about that later.

Patrick took his seat on the northeast side of the sitting area, I took the opposite northwest and we began discussing a wide range of topics concerning the activity in the backyard since I took ownership in 1991 and my extensive studies of paranormal activity there. I asked "Patrick are you ready to check out hell's path?" As one of the best, if not THE best paranormal investigator in the country, he was more than ready. He had his K2 meter in hand which he had modified with a switch to keep finger pressure from dictating possible human movement and error and wanted to find out for himself if there was any validity to all the tales of haunting related to this very beautiful yet mysterious location. We ventured up Hell's Path as I lovingly call it. Ok odd name, but I have my reasons. I told Patrick to stop at the prime location. He did so immediately. I told him here he could ask questions and he did so without hesitation. He guided with explanation that if the spirits lit up the K2 meter once that would be a positive reply and twice would be a negative reply. He began by asking if any spirits were present. He got a positive response. He then asked several more questions. I mentioned that he could ask questions of

Mary and she would probably give him the answers that he sought. Patrick boldly asked Mary just how many spirits were present. The K2 meter was going wild. Patrick smiled and asked her to slow down and that he would need to count how many based on the times she made the K2 light up. Again very quickly it went off, we were both counting frantically and it came to 14. He asked again and to please slow down a bit. Again it was 14. So he had the validation he needed. At this point all I can do is smile. You see as a science based, extremely knowledgeable person, Patrick knew there was no means of electricity so therefore there could be no interference. This in itself is amazing. And no, neither of us had cell phones on or anything that could lead to interference. After a while longer of hypothesizing on what on earth was going on we meandered back down to the circle area. Patrick and I both took our seats just exactly as we'd left them. Zeus of course has been about the whole time but he has bonded with Patrick and chooses to hang out close to him. Patrick and I continue to talk about the activity along hell's path and Zeus gets up rather fast and runs into the woods to the North, then no sooner than you can say "Alabama" we heard something coming from near the house and it was Zeus coming from the opposite direction just slowly walking towards us. At first sight he was about 50 feet away in the opposite direction of the sight of his entry into the woods. Now folks, there is no way in hell that could have happened, but it did, and we both witnessed it. How could Zeus have even done a 180 and made it back, impossible. Great Pyrenees are fast but large, they pant due to their weight and size alone in just a short run. Zeus was not panting. It was as though Zeus just walked lazily *towards us in the opposite direction. Too freaking weird for words, then it gets a bit odder. Ok, you have two very well known paranormal investigators bantering back and forth on what are the odds, how in the world did this happen? Is it theoretically possible? Um, no. There was first, not enough time and secondly no physical signs from Zeus of that type of run, unless of course that was not Zeus, but it was him. When I say, more odd, that is exactly what I mean, things got more odd. I would estimate 20 minutes later, Zeus was laying beside Patrick on the ground close enough that Patrick could pet Zeus's head. Zeus let out a fierce growl. Now folks, Zeus is not a vicious dog. Zeus immediately got up and bolted towards the side yard. Patrick and I both looked at him with amazement, like what the dickens! As we are watching Zeus a type of disk white in color the size of a stop sign but shaped like a home plate on a baseball field comes flying across the yard, and it isn't a Frisbee. Zeus is barking ferociously. The object swoops down toward Zeus, Zeus lunges at it and bites at it and then it does a right bank as it looked as though it had gone through Zeus's head and off it went into the night. Patrick looked at me, I looked back at Patrick and without much delay at all we were both saying, "Did you see that?" I'll leave out many of the explicative's as I know some of you are younger readers, but you get the picture. Two educated adults have just seen something that absolutely is beyond human comprehension. So what was this object? Zeus literally took flight to bite it but he bit right through it. What was it, why was it there and why can't it be explained? I still to this day have been in fear of actually discussing it with more than just a few close friends and colleagues. It happened. I've seen some very strange things out there, some of which I will NEVER disclose but with Patrick's permission I am sharing this event with you. I'm ready and prepared to hear any ideas you might have on this particular event. To be honest, a team that had come to train and investigate this backyard had a team member who had stated he had seen an unidentified flying object on the premises and I have pictures that confirm certain things and other witnesses of such oddities, but having Patrick to witness this was unbelievable timing. It's almost like, ok Deborah you are not crazy, these other people who have seen such things are not crazy, but what is it? I want the answer.*

The Power of the Circle

I'm getting a little personal here but I have an idea but no conclusion that my beliefs may have an affect itself on the backyard. As you know I have a circle or fire area that I built many years ago in the back. I did this of course for the fellowship of the fire during the cool weather but also as an area in which I can give honor to my ancestors and pay homage to my personal beliefs of the elements and such: air, water, earth, fire, and the spirits. I also light a candle for healing. I practice healing, not as an art, but to help others. This is one of those gifts that I have been blessed with. No, I can't heal everything, but there are ways that I can comfort some types of ailments and sometimes eliminate some types of ailments altogether. So the healing candle is important to me. The others I place in there proper areas and honor each. You may call it a Ritual. I call it doing my thing. You may say I'm a devil worshipper, but you could be no more wrong. I don't even believe in the devil. I believe in a higher power. If his name is God, so be it. If his name is Jehovah, so be it. I call him Creator, the creator of all that is beautiful on this earth. We as humans create all that is good or bad by our actions. So personal beliefs out of the way, this is who I am, like me or not. But this circle that I allow to surround me I use to call to all the good spirits for all that I need to continue my faith. I ask for guidance and pray to live a good life, an honest life and never ever hurt anyone maliciously or with content. This day and time when our lives are so fast paced we forget to thank anyone for the blessings that are bestowed on us each and every day. It can be as simple as the smile of child or a life saved from harm. I was raised to be Christian and I feel I am, I simply choose to direct my prayers to the one who leads me through this path of life and hope that through prayer I can accomplish all that I was destined to. My philosophy is simple; if I can help just one person each day of my life then I have met my goals in life. So if I do this by my writing, by my responding to calls of help, by paying attention to my innermost consciousness then I am following that path. If I stray then the Creator will kick start me back with a rude awakening and I'll get it right. When I open my circle I say my prayers to all that is good in this world and hope that I continue to do good for all of mankind and I ask for spiritual guidance. I also ask that all good spirits be allowed to join me. For that I may open up some type of pathway for those entities. It could be my timing, who knows, but I may very well have opened up something very special back there that makes spirits feel comfortable. I become one of the earth...one of the air...one of the water...and one of the fire. It is my special place where all my feelings come forth. It is my special place to find sanctuary in sometimes an unjust world. It is my special place to become one with nature and spiritual activity. No, I'm no heathen. As I stated earlier, I believe in a higher power and I live my life based on truth, honesty and love.

The Empowering Trees

Since I consider myself a glorified tree hugger, this chapter will flow easily for me. I hope. Someone told me once long ago when things are getting to you so badly that you feel like you are about to lose your grip go in the yard or woods somewhere and just sit down with your back touching a tree. Since I'm so curious I did just that. When you lean on that tree its like you are being wrapped in a cocoon of safety, making you feel safe and secure and a little warm and fuzzy. Trees are so alive. Oh to be a tree to live for centuries and see so much of what surrounds you. If trees could talk, what stories would they tell? I refer to some special trees as empowering. Why, you ask? There are a few in the backyard that imamate some type of electrical charge. No, I'm not kidding. I have shared this with a few people. Even one who brought a special rock to be recharged that was used for healing purposes. This emanation of electricity seems to recharge me. I can feel the power of the tree coming slowly through my body it brings inverted chill bumps as this is occurring. It goes from my feet to the top of my head and then reverses and then with no apparent scientific reasoning it begins to swirl around my body. If you can picture the inside of a swirling tornado you can see the wind circulating. This is what it feels like to my body, as though the current is circulating around me. It's the most unusual sensation, and then afterwards, I am revitalized. Some family and friends refer to me as a 'walking tens unit'. They aren't far off. As incredulous as this may sound, it's true. Some of the trees in the backyard are empowering in a very personal yet uncommon way.

Hell's Path

I know many of you wonder why on earth I would name a path behind my house what I did. Here is the only explanation I can give you. I, being sensitive, consider it sometimes a blessing, sometimes a curse. For the most part it is a kind of hell on earth. Why? Being able to see things that others can't, knowing the foreboding feeling of an impending danger to those that you love. Seeing things that make you feel like you should be committed rather than walk about freely because you spend hours, months, and years just trying to learn to cope with the things that enter your mind. This path seems to be a tool that I use to determine whether or not others have those similar types of 'sensitive' abilities. To me we all have the ability, some of us simply choose to ignore them or due to the fact that we are raised with a certain belief structure it is not acceptable to stray from those beliefs. Sometimes these abilities are simply hard to ignore or they will drive you crazy. Acceptance is the key. Acceptance of who you are. I take each and every gift that I have been blessed with and try to use those blessings to help others to understand. I know the path like the back of my hand. I know where you feel certain things, like tingling of your body for example when you get at one location. If you are sensitive you can feel an electrical current flowing and touching you. At another part of this path your heart sinks as you feel the pain of lives lost in ancient times. At one part you can feel eyes watching you and it gives you a kind of creepy feeling. Hell's Path is a training ground and one that I, as a teacher of the paranormal, can pick up on whether or not some are in tune with their own sensitive abilities. I have spent countless hours with many, many people making observations of their feelings and all senses as they walk this path. The path is always open should you choose to walk it.

Sing Louder To Me

So long as you haven't skipped around in this book you understand how I do my circle. The Singing comes from tree frogs, crickets, birds and other wildlife. When the moon is full this tends to happen more than any other time of the month. I think that nature must really come more alive at this point in time. I have completed many a prayer session and sat out in the backyard for hours on end and had the ability to ask the voices of nature to sing louder and they do. Amazing huh? Ask those who know me if this is not a true statement. Is it coincidental, yes maybe the first or second times, but let's go with hundreds of times. Also this works on a reverse manner as well. Recently I was with around ten or so investigators out in the backyard and a group of coyotes were going crazy across the road. You could tell they had to be a half mile or so away. The barking almost got to the point of an endless scream. I spoke up. I put my hand up and said "Listen "and "Hush"...they became silent immediately. This adds to my curiosity as to "Am I responsible for unusual things that happen here?" Give some thought to that please.

Twas the Night Before Halloween

Ok, so the name of the chapter is kind of lame, but the events were anything but. As you can guess we were out in the famous backyard enjoying a fire and a night of fun. My husband and I and another pal were taking turns taking random photos of each other and also looking for anything paranormal we might come up with. Taking pictures of fire is always a hoot for my husband; you can see so many different things in it, just like looking at puffy clouds in the sky. Well this night was no different we thought until after Halloween.

I had purchased a Halloween costume to wear from a local retailer, costume rental location. A very nice costume indeed, Maid Marian style with all the accessories to the tune of well over 100.00 and it had been used a few years, LOL. It was a lovely durable cloth purple gown with gold filament trim. The accessories consisted of arm guard made of purple cloth, a silky long scarf with a gold neckband and a crown made of gold cloth that had a V that came down onto my forehead. Posh eh? I went all out. But remember this was the night before, jeans on, sweatshirt the casual wear. Well we wrapped up the evening and headed into the house and to my computer I went to upload the photos of the night. Once a paranormal investigator, always a paranormal investigator I say. Get those pictures up so you can review, even if they were just for fun. Low and behold but what does appear, a woman wearing my costume that is yet hanging in the bedroom waiting for me to wear it the next night? Talk about shock. Well not only is she wearing my costume but she looks like me but the guy standing next to her is not my husband. He looks like something from back a long time ago. You look and tell me what you see.

Talk about a shocker, seriously. How on earth did the lady on the left know what I was planning to wear the next night? What on earth has that man on the right got on his head? It looks like a huge metal on his forehead. Just another mystery to add to the many of the haunted backyard I guess. Well needless to say, I wore it the next night. I sure did!!

Spirits Riding Through

I've certainly heard of taking a ride through the park but this one still leaves me a little curious, in fact, very curious. Normally you capture in photos still actions but it's rare to capture something that is actually riding on something with wheels. I've laughed many times about this particular capture. So much that I figured everyone else would as well and the fear of ridicule has kept me from posted it on my web site so I snuck it in as an animation on the front page for a while. This young man has dark hair with a bowl type hair cut and could be riding on any number of things, possibly a bicycle or motorcycle or even a tricycle of sorts. To tell you the truth I'm just not sure, but you have a voice. Email me at nealparasociety@aol.com if you think you can figure this one out.

Demonic Banishing

There came a time in the house when things were going a bit array. So a decision was made to do a banishing. A banishing is generally performed before the cleansing ritual. Its purpose is to cleanse the area in my case the house—whether it be a room or a haunted location—all those elements that might interfere with the normal day to day routine. Banishing consists of removing all negative energy or negative spiritual activity from this time my home to get it back in proper order. Things were becoming misplaced. Doors were opening and closing on their own, loud banging on the back door leading to the backyard.

Banishing rituals may also be performed for their own sake. This can be done for several reasons—to cleanse a room or home, to eliminate negative or unwanted energy, or to simply calm and balance the mind. Many people have to do banishing ceremonies daily, thank the creator I'm not one who does. I gathered together the NAPS team at that time. Three of us gathered the tools needed for a banishing ceremony and began "pushing" the negative energy out of the house. Well as any good paranormal investigator would do we had cameras rolling. You will not believe what appeared as we had walked through the house and had gotten to a window facing the backyard. Look for yourself. I see a man, very scruffy. Actually he's not wearing much clothing and he's right next to the window with a not so nice look on his face. What do you see?

What transpired worked. The air was lighter and paranormal activity slowed down.

When the Candles were Lit

This photo was taken by Reese Christian while she was here on a visit and investigation of the backyard. Reese has been studying various types of rituals and she had asked would I do "what I do" to observe. I complied. Reese uses a regular 35 mm camera. You actually have to get your photos developed. She captured this that night. Could be explainable but it is another for curiosities sake.

I'm Watching You

I know we talk about Orbs a lot as what they can be whether it is dust, moisture, pollen or any number of things. This particular night I was working with my dousing rods out in the backyard. We had been to a location earlier and then went out back for a little training. I'm a trainer, my team knows it, if you aren't willing to open your mind and learn then hanging with me is no fun. I'm going to share with you two photographs taken in succession so you can see this "thing" watching me. I say watching me because of the angle in which it hangs, literally. Dust should have flown on by, water should have dissipated and pollen should be lying on the ground by now. So you see what you think.

Deb with Naps Robert

Faces Watch Too!

This one I've tried to debunk. I know who was in the backyard. I know we had one person with blue on but they were not in the wood line at the time. Also that person wears glasses, can't see two feet in front of them without them. Also they were male and this illusion, entity or whatever appears female. There is nothing there that would create that blue color. So I now throw this one at you for you to see.

Are Children More Aware?

I'm sure that some of you have children, grandchildren, nieces or nephews that had stories relayed to you about their having imaginary friends at some point in time. This was just an afternoon of play in the backyard with friends and family. My little sweetie was just chattering away to someone and this picture was taken. I'll let you see the whole picture and then isolate and enlarge the orb. The only thing I find odd about this standard orb (if there is a standard) is the side that is broken and it appears to have a small formation in it. This is just another oddity to share. Indeed I do feel that as children we do have abilities to see and hear things that as adults we tune to hone out.

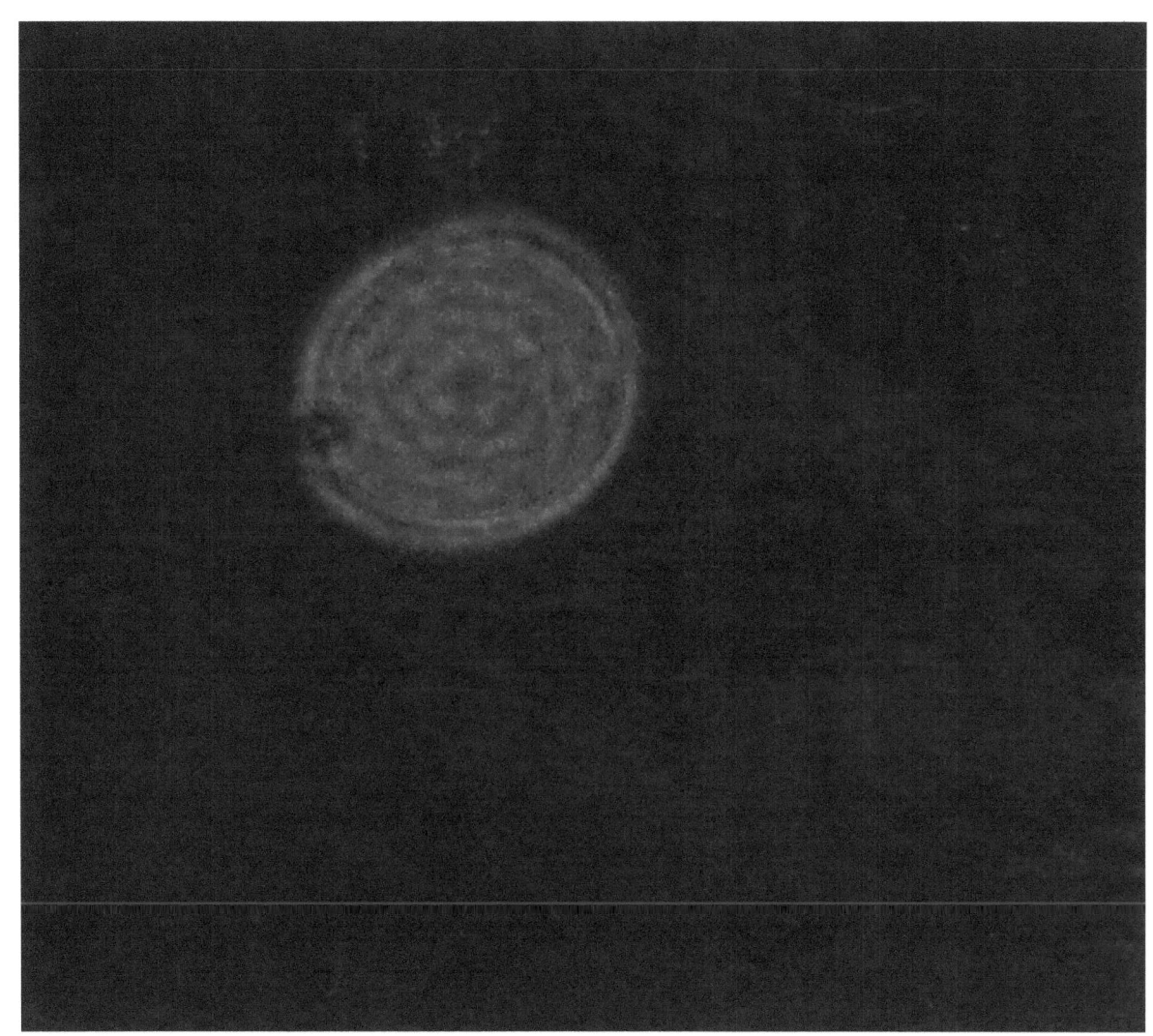

Deborah's Ghostly Family

This is one extremely weird photo. I know, weird is not a good term, but under the circumstances this capture was on the back on the back of my head. I'm wearing a ball cap as you will see but there is a either a photograph image or some type of almost portrait type thing on the there. I don't recognize these people. My son took a look at it and said one of them actually favors his Grandpa Collard. Then my grandson took a look, he's 5, and he said I see a man, someone wearing a black cape and hood and a brat. I see a man, a woman slightly looking outside of a hooded cape and a child in her arms. After the photo was taken I looked on the back of my head in a mirror and nothing, absolutely nothing could have attributed to this image. I'd love to know what other people see. This was just your average night of backyard adventure. Here is the photograph for your viewing.

Orbs that Trail Along

Have you ever captured a photograph of what appears to be an Orb in movement? Well this one seems to be moving right along. Nice capture I think of the movement. Some people would say this orb is more of a vortex than an orb. I'm holding back my decision. Here is the photograph. First you will see the original and then next a zoom in of the photograph.

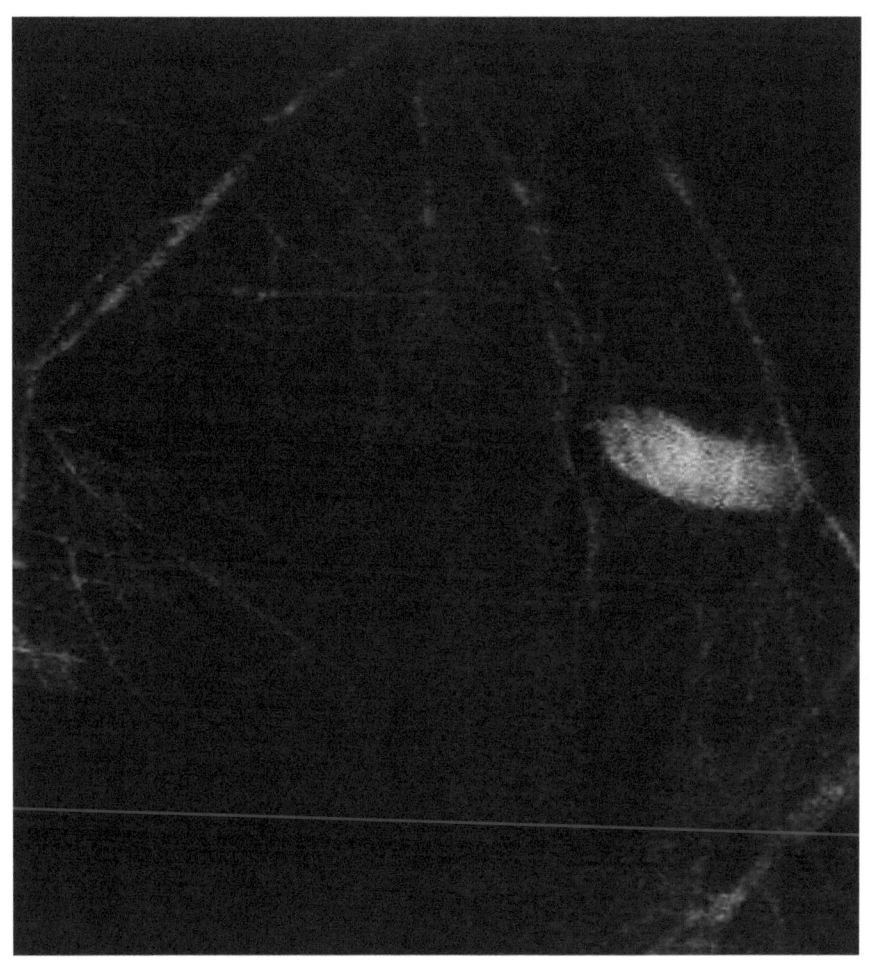

Red Orbs

Red orbs are sometimes an oddity for me to see. Sometimes we capture them, sometimes we don't. I have a feeling that the red ones are more of an energy orb. That is my opinion. Also these are the ones I feel have the ability to increase the possibility of something manifesting itself to us as paranormal investigators. Here are two photos back to back for you to note the changes in the red orb.

Red Orb – 2, next frame

Hexagon Shaped Orb

I don't know about you but I've not seen many hexagon orbs in my career. But this night was an exception, clearly being able to see the orb or whatever we should call it with a face nearby. The photograph tells all.

(Mist)ical Photos

Some nights when the backyard comes alive strange mists form. Not black, not white but beautiful shades of purple. I'd like to share some photos taken in succession that show you just how it happens. The backyard forest is very much alive!

The last four photos were taken in December 2007. The temperature was 46 degrees; winds were at 3 miles per hour (variable), 10 mile visibility, dew point at 30.7 and clear. There was no fire burning anywhere. There was no one allowed with a cigarette. No reason for the mist. We even attempted to recreate with exhaling in front of the camera. No re-creation of the photos was possible. Interesting I say!

History Section

I Ask Myself Why?

I didn't want to bore you with the history of my home before I gave you the toe curling things that have occurred here in the backyard area. But now that you have been told "some" of the stories regarding paranormal activity back there I will.

I bought this home back in 1991. The story of how I obtained it is still kind of amazing to me. My husband and I had been renting for several years and moving about with the kids and I came across a "House for Sale by Owner" in the local newspaper and the good thing was it was only two miles from where we worked.

The house is lake view and we both love the lake so it was beginning to sound very perfect. My husband said there was no way we could afford a house in that neighborhood and that was that!! Well… I decided to call the owners and ask could I see the house. They were kind enough to drive up the very next day and let me do the first walk through. When the front door was unlocked and I stepped into the living room it was home. I knew it. I really didn't need to look any farther but of course I did. Then we went outside and I looked around the grounds. The grounds just screamed "me"! When the gentleman explained how far back in the woods the property went I was amazed. It's a good size plot of land. And then I asked 'How much do you have to have down?" He said ten percent is what we would like to have. I swallowed deeply wondering just where in the dickens I could come up with that kind of money. I was working two jobs at that time and one of them was sales sooooo I might be able to make this work. I gave the man a check for earnest money. I told him to please give me seven days to come up with the needed down payment. He and his wife both smiled and said OK. So for the next seven days I prayed for cash sales at my sales job because I got a 12% commission. The owner of the company told me she would pay as long as all checks written by purchasers were good all my commissions on Friday. Pop, bam, zowwie!! I was able to obtain all the capital I needed in five days of sales plus a little money I had in the bank. That was a miracle in itself. During this time they had done the proverbial credit check and I'd slid by that one without a problem. I didn't bother to ask about anyone having died here, that wasn't an issue. It had a new roof, new central heat and air and had been well maintained although you could tell it had not been lived in for a while. So I dragged my husband to the lawyer's office to sign papers. He truly did not want to, but he did because he knew I would without him. I was already attached to it. The children blossomed. They had their forever home. I never knew it would mean as much to them as it did to me. But it did and still does.

Well we got moved into the house, got the kids settled into their new schools and were a hop, skip & jump to work. With the exception of my second job as an RN, I had to relocate to a hospital closer to home.

We had been here maybe a week and a neighbor who was a sister to the previous owner's son told me more about this house and property. It seemed her sister had died here. She had built the house new and lived here until death. She explained to me how much her sister loved this home and the grounds. Lights were going off now!

I was sitting on the sofa unloading some boxes and heard someone walking through the kitchen. Eh, I was the only one home. Then I saw a shadow of a small lady walked back out of the kitchen and down the hall. Ok, this house was going to be haunted by the lady who built it, but you know, that was going to be fine by me. We would learn to cohabitate. The floor in the kitchen had a worn path, evidently she made that walk many times a day and I wasn't about to stop her now.

Just as soon as I got through getting things unloaded and in place I would spend every waking moment in the backyard. I made flower beds, a rock path and planted trees. I would work tirelessly back there. I'd say that was the best escape and therapy for relaxation I could have ever found.

The kids grew up, I got older, the family grew and some of our favorite pets passed. But one thing is for sure the backyard has remained the same, a gathering place.

This is a weird story times two. I've gotten whirlwind ideas about moving to another property I own and decided to sell this house twice. The first time my youngest daughter Ricci threw a fit. She was terribly upset that I would even consider it and she didn't even live here anymore. Her problem was she'd planted a magnolia tree in the front yard and granted it is beautiful but she could always plant another wherever I moved. Well it seems it didn't just upset her. I decided to have some repairs done to make it more sellable. The place needed new field lines, it was time. So I made the call and had the contractor come in to do it. Appointment made! Well when he came to my door and asked me to show him the property lines I grabbed on some shoes and out I went. I noticed the realtor had been by and put up the For Sale sign. As I neared the edge of the property I stepped in a hole. Now granted I know every square inch of this place and there should not have been a hole there. Needless to say there was and I found it. Down my right foot went into the hole and down I went to. The contractor who is an old dear friend said, "What are you doing Deborah?" Me in total pain smiled and said I've fallen and I really don't think I can get up. Believe it or not he began to tell me about a remembrance of turning over his ankle at a high school football game and how he continued to play even though he was hurt. I hushed him kind of quickly when I said I think I'm about to pass out, I may have broken my leg. When he tried to help me up and he saw my leg he hollered for help and another fellow got a porch chair, they sat me in it and took me up to the yard in front of the house. He was going in to call an ambulance. I said no, just call Greg at the store, he'll come get me. Well I never shed a tear until they laid me in the back seat of our car. Then I went at it. Greg fussed about why I didn't call an ambulance. I told him he'd be quicker. When we got to the Emergency Room the doctor after having sent me back for X-rays said you have quite an unusual break. It was my fibula and it looked to him like it had been cut completely into with a butter knife. Oh well, at least it wasn't displaced. I determined it was just simply an accident. The For Sale listing was for three months. I was trapped inside for six weeks and told the realtor no one could look at the house until I was a bit mended. Then the realtor called and had someone that really was interested. Well I had to use a wheelchair at times because the leg wasn't healing properly. A clean break, it should! So to the house comes the realtor to show someone around. After they left I decided I would make some soup. My husband had asked me time and time again not to cook just make something like a sandwich for lunch and he'd make dinner when he got in. Well not this day, I was determined. A possible buyer! As I had poured the hot soup into a bowl and was about to lower it to my lap something knocked it right out of my hand and poured hot soup all over my bare legs. Ouch! I called a neighbor who is also a nurse and she brought up some burn cream, I didn't have any. Geez, second degree burns and a broken leg, I was a piece of work I tell you.

The house was NOT being nice to me. I thought about it a while, then I prayed about it and then made a choice. Just maybe the house didn't want me to sell it either. By now I was ready to try anything to keep from getting hurt anymore. I called the realtor, told him the house listing needs to come down. He was a tad bit upset seeing as how it looked like he was going to get a hefty commission. The next Thursday I had an appointment with my orthopedic. He was shocked; I actually had some bone growth. I could finally get up on crutches. Coincidence, I think not. Why you say?

Two years later, I made the decision again to sell the house. A fellow who worked for the realtor came out to set the For Sale sign. He left. I was cleaning the kitchen, bent over to tie the garbage back and OOPS! Pain! I called the husband crying and said I need you to take me to the doctor. He said do you have an appointment. I replied just get here now please. I made him drive past the local hospital and go on to Huntsville to my Orthopedic. Thank god the doctor was willing to see me after blessing me out for not going to an emergency room. A piece of my iliac spine had literally just broken off!! I told my husband right then and there the house does not want to be sold. If we sell it, the damn thing will kill me. So down came the sign. Not a problem since then. When I was able to get around which was in just a few days I walked out in the backyard and asked for a truce. Now I face another dilemma. I would very much like to live at my cabin on the lakefront. How the hell do I get this house to agree? I know you think this is the oddest thing in the world and maybe a rash of coincidence but I believe you can understand where I'm coming from. My house must love me ☺

The backyard never lets me down. It's very predictable. I have a tree that exerts more healing energy than you could imagine. I have an area where it feels like there is a magnetic energy field that you really shouldn't go past. I have all kinds of spiritual entities that come around following the nine pm hour. Good thing I'm a paranormal investigator, good thing I have my certification in parapsychological studies, good thing I'm into ghosts don't you think?

Tidbits of Information of Meltonsville

Location of the Haunted Backyard

Small inhabited community

Coordinates 34.433 degrees N – 86.183 degrees W

Located in Marshall County, AL

650 Feet above Sea Level

Surrounded by the Tennessee River

Meltonsville, once known as Melton's Village was a small Creek Settlement that was established right around the time of the Creek War of 1813 with permission of the Cherokee who lived here. The village stood less than 1 mile from this home. The location of the village is still known as "Old Village Ford". It was named Meltonsville due to its chief Charles Melton who was an old Indian. The trail from Gunter's Village to Coosada came to here. The post office of Meltonsville was named after Melton. The old post office structure is about 500-600 feet from this property.

This village was considered an Upper Creek Village. The Upper Creek (Red Sticks) opposed the take over from while men while the Lower Creek are said to have agreed with a peaceful transition and actually fought along side the soldiers.

It is said Tali was an ancient town that was traveled through by Desoto's expedition July 10, 1540. Tali was located on McKee's Island in the Tennessee River near Guntersville. Many burials plots, Indian villages were buried under the waters of the Tennessee here when the Guntersville Dam was built. The chief of Tali sent the women and children to meet Desoto's Cavalry. When the Spanish expedition exited Tali on July 11, 1540 the Cherokee gave them two warriors and four women to use as servants.

They say most likely that from about 1500 until well along in the seventeenth century, perhaps to its very close, the Koasati lived upon Tennessee River. There is good reason to think that they are the Coste, Acoste, or Costehe of De Soto's chroniclers whose principal village was upon an island in the river, Pine Island. Pine Island is directly across the river from this property on the back side. The Main Channel of the Tennessee would have separated the properties by about 1 mile. This is also mentioned of them in the narrative of Pardo's expedition of 1567 inland Santa Elena, and by the entries made on maps published early in the eighteenth century this tribe seems to have occupied the same position when the French and English made their settlements in the Southeast. About that time they were probably joined by a family tribe Kaskinampo. Not long after they had become known to the Whites, a large part of the Koasati migrated south and established the tribe at or near Pine Island.

As you can see, this small community was by far inhabited mainly by Native Americans. I live on a peninsula. This was ideal for the Indians to be able to see up and down the river and watch for impending trouble. Meltonsville encompasses on a few square miles but important ones. The area is rich in food supply, planting season and harvest times are long, fish are abundant, deer and all types of wildlife. To me the most important asset is the water. This peninsula would have been a perfect place for battle. I have no documentation only feelings that this indeed occurred many times over. With such a rich history of lives lived, lives lost, sometimes untimely there is a true opportunity for all the paranormal activity found here.

As I sit and write tonight the wind howls and water white caps, it's as though the trees speak. I probably should be outside but I'm ducking out since the trees may decide to throw a limb at me. I'm going to close for now hoping that each reader has enjoyed viewing the photo evidence that I've put out for examination. As always I will continue to follow my destiny seeking out many more Haunted Southern Nights. You see each night I spend at home is indeed "another Haunted Southern Night."

Please continue to join me in my quest for the truth; I know it's out there. Until next time my friends.

As Time Passes So Do Lives.........

Deborah Collard, RN

Founder: North-Eastern Alabama Paranormal Society

Certification in Parapsychological Studies

Member of the Parapsychological Association

Member Alabama State Board of Nursing

Tribal Member: United Cherokee Ani-Yun-Wiya Nation

Host of NAPS Live Radio "Haunted Southern Nights"©

Author: "Haunted Southern Nights, Vol. 1, Ghost Hunting, The Basics+©

Contact info:

www.nealparasociety.com

www.myspace.com/nealparasociety

www.blogtalkradio.com/naps

Deborah, who is Cherokee by blood, enjoys reaching back into the past to connect her with the spiritual world. The way she celebrates this passion is through her studies of the paranormal. Deborah considers herself an 'oldie' in this venue, knowing that 30 years ago the only tools she used to investigate with were her flashlight and whomever she could drag along with her to see if she could find answers to the many questions that wandered through her mind. Did the spirits of those who had passed still have a grasp on the earth via earthbound spirits? Was there truly a form of life after death? Were there those who chose not to leave for reasons unknown? Today she enjoys her life as a wife, mother, and even a Nana! Her quest for answers has never ceased. As technology progressed so did she and many years later has a very solid team of paranormal investigators. The Team is NAPS – North-Eastern Alabama Paranormal Society. NAPS was officially formed and being sought out to do investigations in 2004. If asked she will tell you NAPS is her family. Deborah teaches a paranormal workshop, also does lectures and panels on the paranormal. It is important to her that ghost hunters know just what they are doing and the proper way to do it!

In January 2007 Deborah and NAPS became a viable part of OmegaCon. OmegaCon promises to be the greatest sci/fi, fantasy and paranormal convention to ever come to the State of Alabama. OmegaCon will be held in Birmingham, Alabama on March 14-16, 2008.

Now NAPS is taking it one step further with the guidance of OmegaCon Productions. Haunted Southern Nights was always a dream to Deborah but OmegaCon Productions is making it a reality. In July, NAPS began filming a series of paranormal investigations in some of the hottest locations in the South. "Haunted Southern Nights" is scheduled to be premiered in March at OmegaCon.

In October 2007, Deborah authored her first book "Haunted Southern Nights Volume 1 Ghost Hunting, the Basics+". The new book entails how

Deborah Collard has been aggressively seeking answers to paranormal activity since being a teenager. Deborah uses both scientific methods as well as sensitive methods to attempt to determine the evidentiary proof of spiritual activity. Seeking the clues to life after death is something that we all look for. This book will begin you on a path to develop your paranormal investigative skills and to understand why people choose to follow this path. Many questions asked, many answered in Haunted Southern Nights. You be the judge.

Deborah continued her studies in the paranormal by completing post-secondary education offered at the HCH Institute under the tutelage of Loyd Auerbach and received a certification in Parapsychological Studies. For the past several years Deborah has trained many paranormal investigators and continues to lecture and panel in her region on the paranormal.

Deborah hosts NAPS Live Radio "Haunted Southern Nights" along with her friend and colleague Nathan Levan, NAPS investigator and VP of OmegaCon. Tuesday nights are very much looked forward to. Deborah seems to never meet a stranger or a ghost she can't be friends with.

www.ingramcontent.com/pod-product-compliance
Lightning Source LLC
Chambersburg PA
CBHW041831300426
44111CB00002B/49